Amazing Animals

ALLIGATORS

Multiplication

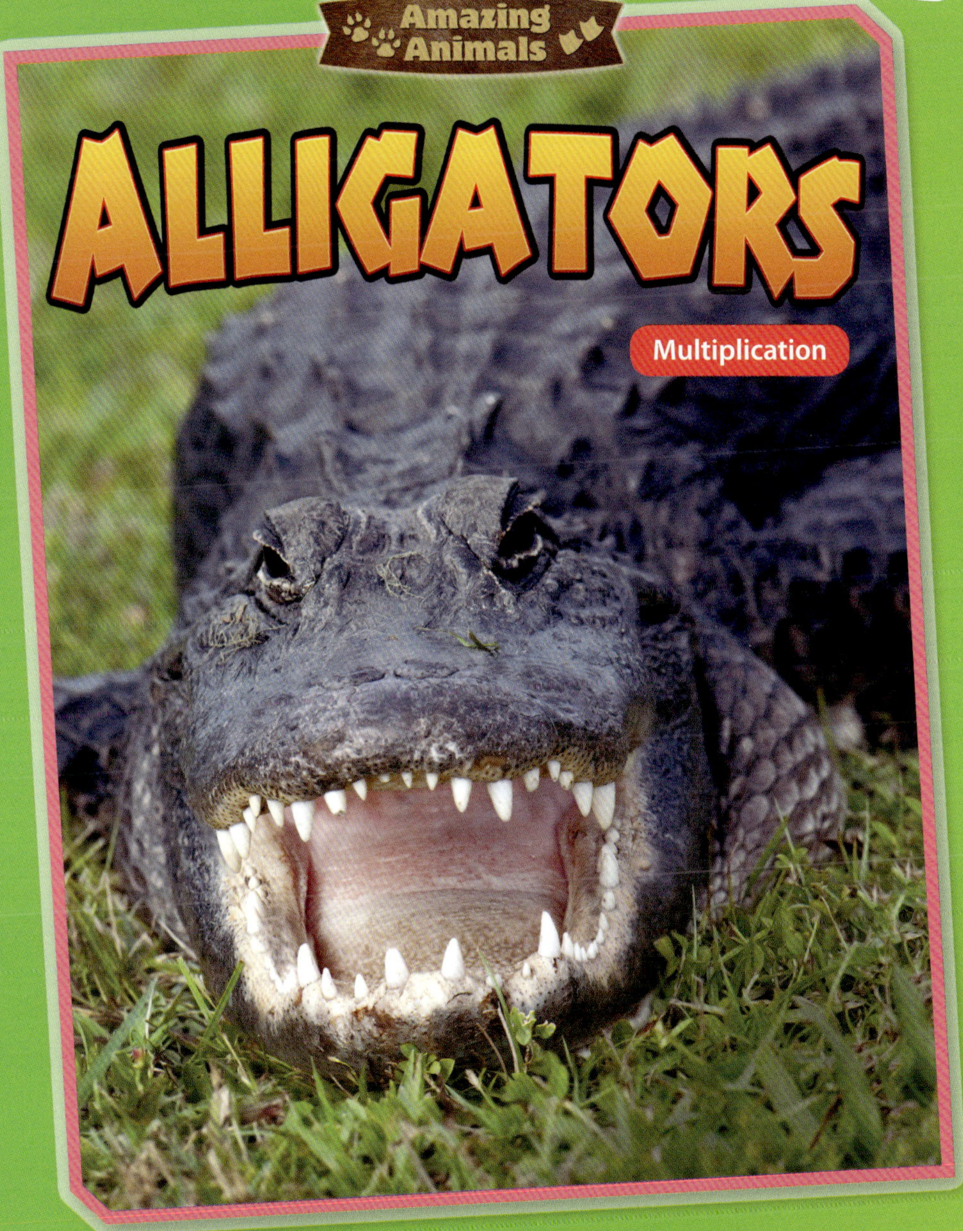

Darlene Misconish Tyler, M.Ed.

Consultants

Michele Ogden, Ed.D
Principal
Irvine Unified School District

Colleen Pollitt, M.A.Ed.
Math Support Teacher
Howard County Public Schools

Publishing Credits

Rachelle Cracchiolo, M.S.Ed., *Publisher*
Conni Medina, M.A.Ed., *Managing Editor*
Dona Herweck Rice, *Series Developer*
Emily R. Smith, M.A.Ed., *Series Developer*
Diana Kenney, M.A.Ed., NBCT, *Content Director*
Stacy Monsman, M.A., *Editor*
Kevin Panter, *Graphic Designer*

Image Credits: p. 12 AP Photo/Al.com, Sharon Steinmann; pp. 16–17 Henry, P./picture alliance/Arco Images G/Newscom; p. 17 James P. Rod/Science Source; pp. 18–19, back cover George Shelley/Getty Images; p. 19 Michael Patrick O'Neill/Alamy Stock Photo; p. 24 AP Photo/The Beaumont Enterprise, Dave Ryan; p. 26 imageBROKER/Alamy Stock Photo; all other images from iStock and/or Shutterstock.

Library of Congress Cataloging-in-Publication Data

Names: Tyler, Darlene Misconish, author.
Title: Alligators / Darlene Misconish Tyler, M.Ed.
Description: Huntington Beach, CA : Teacher Created Materials, [2018] | Series: Amazing animals | Audience: Grade 4 to 6. | Includes index.
Identifiers: LCCN 2017011829 (print) | LCCN 2017014383 (ebook) | ISBN 9781480759305 (eBook) | ISBN 9781425855482 (paperback)
Subjects: LCSH: Alligators--Juvenile literature.
Classification: LCC QL666.C925 (ebook) | LCC QL666.C925 T97 2018 (print) | DDC 597.98/4--dc23
LC record available at https://lccn.loc.gov/2017011829

Teacher Created Materials
5301 Oceanus Drive
Huntington Beach, CA 92649-1030
http://www.tcmpub.com

ISBN 978-1-4258-5548-2

Printed by 51250
PO48266 / Printed in USA

Table of Contents

Powerful Reptiles

The air is hot and sticky. You sweat as you walk along a river in Florida. Suddenly, you hear a hiss from off to your left. As you peer through the tall grass surrounding the river, you see a pair of eyes flash in the water. You watch the alligator as you back away slowly. After a few steps, you hear a loud snap and you turn to run!

American alligator

Chinese alligator

Alligators can be scary, but they are amazing creatures. There are two **species** of alligators in the world. American alligators are the largest **reptiles** in North America. Chinese alligators are smaller and can only be found along the Yangtze (YANG-SEE) River.

Alligators are very powerful reptiles. Their size and strength are massive. They use their strong tails to defend themselves. Their tails also help them push through water. They use their teeth and powerful jaws to clamp down on **prey**. Their teeth are specially shaped to rip food into smaller chunks. But, they often choose to just swallow the prey whole!

Alligators aren't the only reptiles that live in water. Crocodiles lurk there, too. They look very similar at first glance. Most people can't tell them apart. But, they are different in many ways. First, alligators have U-shaped snouts. Crocodiles, on the other hand, have V-shaped snouts. Secondly, an alligator's top jaw is wider than its bottom jaw. When its mouth is closed, you can't see any of its teeth. When a crocodile's mouth is shut, the teeth from its jaw stick out the sides of its mouth. Some people think this makes them look like they are smiling. Finally, the webbing on their back feet is also a clue. Crocodiles have much more webbing than alligators.

Maybe you can't get close enough to check a crocodile's snout and feet. In that case, looking at the color of their bodies might help. Crocodiles tend to look lighter than alligators. But the color of the water they are in can change that. So, the easiest way to tell them apart might be where they live. Crocodiles can be found everywhere except Europe and Antarctica. But alligators are only found in North America and China.

LET'S EXPLORE MATH

Suppose that a scientist studying alligators knows there are about 238 alligators living in a nearby swampy area. If the alligator population doubles, how many alligators will there be?

crocodile
alligator

Alligator Traits

Alligators may not live all over the world. But, they have been around for over 150 million years. That means they roamed the earth at the same time as dinosaurs! They have special traits that have helped them survive for such a long time.

Many of these traits can be found on their heads. Adults have between 72 and 80 teeth at one time. As old teeth wear out, new teeth grow in. During its lifetime, an alligator can go through almost 3,000 teeth. These teeth are used to rip and tear prey before swallowing. An alligator's eyes, ears, and nose are on top of its head so it can search for its next meal at the water's surface. Alligators also have special valves in their throats called **glottis** valves. These close so they don't swallow water. This comes in handy when they drag land animals underwater to drown them. All of these traits combine to make alligators great hunters.

But alligators do have one limitation. They can only live in freshwater. They do not have salt glands. This means they cannot filter salt from their bodies. So, ocean swimmers can rest easy knowing they won't spot an alligator coming toward them.

An alligator opens wide, showing off its teeth and powerful jaws.

An alligator swims along the water's surface in Everglades National Park, Florida.

LET'S EXPLORE MATH

An American alligator can have up to 80 teeth in its mouth at one time. Complete the bar models to help you answer the questions.

1. If there are 3 alligators on a riverbank, how many teeth do they have in all?
2. If there are 2 times as many alligators along a lake as there are on the riverbank, how many teeth do they have altogether?

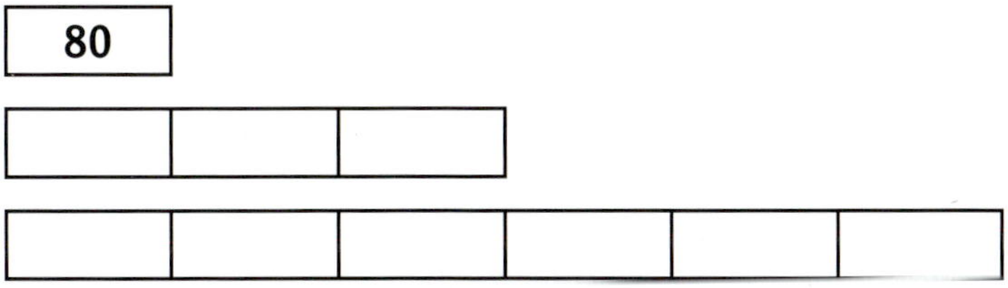

An adult alligator reaches for a turtle.

An alligator warms its body in the sun.

Ocean swimmers may not be on an alligator's menu, but many other animals are. When alligators are young, they are not as strong. So, they can only eat things that are easy to catch. Young alligators eat bugs, fish, and frogs. As they get bigger, so does their food. Adults eat turtles, deer, and even other alligators. They use their strong jaws to crush bones. They can even crack the hard shells of turtles. Adults can digest anything they swallow.

Alligators are cold-blooded creatures. This means their body temperature is based on how cold or hot it is around them. When they are cold, they rest in the sun. When they are hot, they dive deep into cold waters. They do not use energy from food to warm their bodies like mammals do. So, adults only need to eat about once a week in the wild. You definitely do not want to cross the path of a hungry alligator on feeding day!

Alligators use their weight to help them hunt. American alligators can weigh up to 600 pounds (272 kilograms). The heaviest ever caught weighed over 1,000 lbs. (454 kg). That is half of a **ton**! Scientists were stunned. They found a 100 lb. (45 kg) deer in its stomach. The alligator had swallowed it whole!

Alligators are not only heavy. They are also long. Chinese alligators grow from 3 feet (1 meter) to 5 feet (1.5 meters) long. American alligators are even bigger. They can be 6 ft. (2 m) to 12 ft. (4 m) long. The longest one on record was over 15 ft. (5 m)!

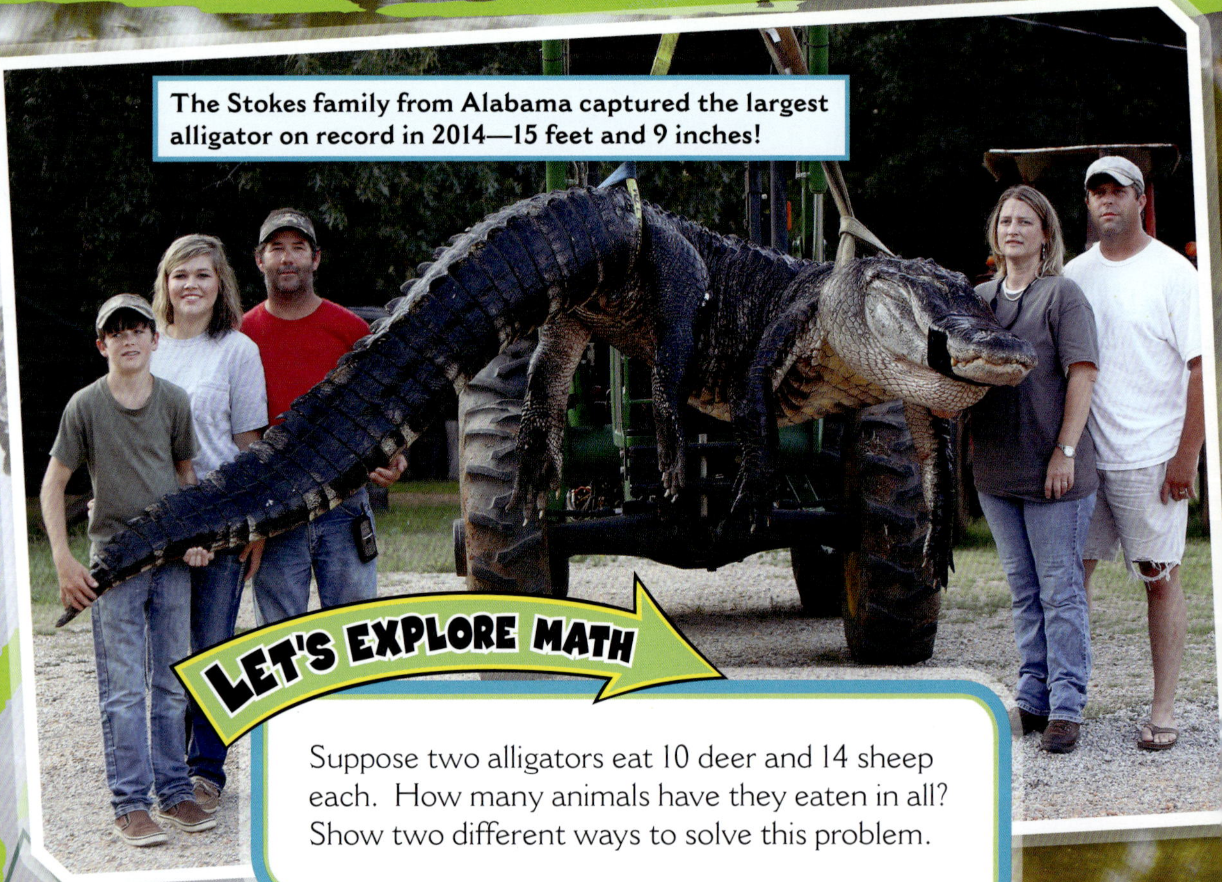

The Stokes family from Alabama captured the largest alligator on record in 2014—15 feet and 9 inches!

LET'S EXPLORE MATH

Suppose two alligators eat 10 deer and 14 sheep each. How many animals have they eaten in all? Show two different ways to solve this problem.

An alligator's tail alone is half of its total length. Alligators use their tails to help them catch prey. On land, they cannot run fast for very long. But in the water, their tails help them reach speeds of up to 20 miles per hour (32 kilometers per hour). Their tails also help them perform a move called the death roll. First, they bite into a large animal. Then, they spin in circles until a chunk rips off. Between death rolls, long bodies, and crushing weight, it's no wonder that alligators have been around for so long!

An alligator family glides through a river.

Living the Wild Life

Alligators as a species have been around for millions of years. But alligators' life spans are not nearly that long. An alligator in the wild can live for up to 50 years. Even though mothers stay with their young for at least six months, it is still dangerous in the wild. Eight out of every 10 alligators in the wild die young. But if they survive, they can defend themselves against most **predators**.

In **captivity**, alligators can live to be 60 to 80 years old. They live longer since they are safer from threats. And, since humans feed them, they do not have to hunt for food. But in captivity, animals are kept in small spaces. They can get bored and lonely.

There are good and bad sides to living in the wild. But there is one type of alligator that is better off living in zoos and farms. Rare white alligators find it hard to survive in the wild. The sun is harsh on their fair skin. And they are very easy for predators to spot. In fact, there are only 12 left on Earth!

white alligator

LET'S EXPLORE MATH

Imagine an alligator lived in the wild for 25 years and a rare white alligator lived in captivity for 75 years. How many times longer did the white alligator live?

1. Write a multiplication equation to represent the situation. Use a □ for the unknown factor.
2. Solve the problem and explain your answer.

This white alligator lives in an enclosure to protect it from direct sunlight.

Hatchlings

Alligators begin their lives in eggs. Many animals, such as adult alligators, eat eggs as part of their diet. So, it is up to the mother to protect them. Females start building nests in early summer. They build their nests with sticks, leaves, and mud to keep the eggs hidden and safe from predators.

A female alligator protects her nest from predators.

Mothers cover the eggs and guard them for the next 70 days. The temperature of the nest controls whether the **hatchlings** will be male or female. Warmer nests often lead to males. Cooler nests often result in females.

Females usually lay between 10 and 60 eggs at a time. But some lay up to 90 eggs! Mothers lay many eggs because other animals may steal and eat the eggs from the nest. Or, the mother might crush some eggs as she tries to defend them. And others might be swept away by floods. It is very hard for the mother to protect them all.

By the time the eggs are ready to hatch, the baby hatchlings have grown a tooth on top of their snouts. They use that tooth to crack open the egg. Then, they make a high-pitched chirping noise. This is their way of telling their mother they are ready to come out. The mother alligator clears off the top of the nest so they can make their way out.

A hatchling emerges from an egg.

As they leave the nest, hatchlings move to the water with their mother. There, they live in pods, or small groups. Hatchlings start hunting the day they are born. They find easy prey in the water, such as insects, shrimp, and small fish. But it is a very dangerous time for them. They are still weak and easy for predators to catch and eat. Most of the young alligators will die before they reach adulthood.

Alligator hatchlings hide in water plants in a Florida river.

Adults

Young alligators face many threats in the wild. But, some of them survive and become adults.

Alligators live in rivers, lakes, swamps, and marshes. They like places where the water is **murky**. The dark water helps them sneak up on their prey. It also helps them hide from predators.

There are over five million alligators living in the southern United States alone. Over a million of those live in Florida. You can spot them in many places. But, if you want to see one up close, the Everglades is the place to go. There, you can ride an **airboat** through the tall grass. And if you look down, you might just spot a pair of eyes peeking up at you.

Tourists look for alligators as they ride an airboat in the Everglades.

LET'S EXPLORE MATH

Suppose there are 4 alligators living along a waterway in the Everglades. Each alligator weighs about 525 pounds. Complete the area model to show how much the alligators weigh altogether.

$$525 \times 4 = \_\_\_\_\_\_$$

×	500 +	20 +	5
4			

Helping One Another

Alligators can be both predator and prey. They are hunters and also hunted. Yet, humans are their biggest threat. Some people hunt them and sell their skin and meat. Humans have also ruined much of their **habitat**. When people build new homes on land, alligators have less space to live. Sometimes, they wander out of the water and enter cities. This can be very dangerous for people and small pets. A dog is no match for a hungry alligator! Some of them have even been caught climbing fences. That is not something most people want to see out their windows!

Alligators used to be **endangered**. People thought they would become **extinct**. But the alligator population has grown in recent years. So, they are not in as much danger now. But we still need to help protect them.

fried alligator

alligator skin shoes

LET'S EXPLORE MATH

In the past, some alligator habitats were being destroyed at a rate of 105 square kilometers per year.

1. About how many square kilometers would be destroyed in 3 years? Estimate by rounding the number of square kilometers to the nearest hundred. Then, find an exact solution.
2. How many square kilometers would be destroyed after 7 years? Show your strategy for finding the solution.

An alligator swims behind a neighborhood.

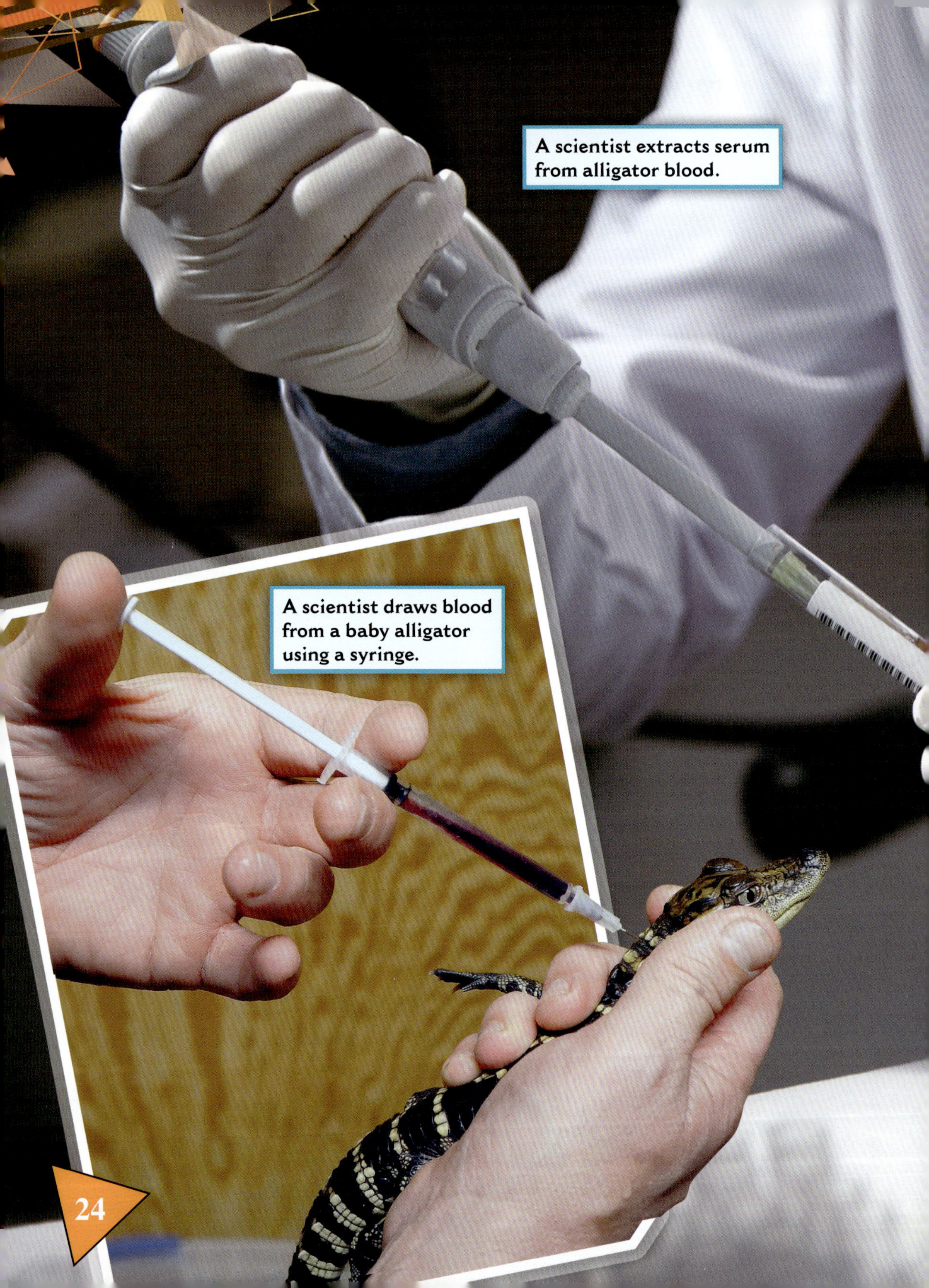

A scientist extracts serum from alligator blood.

A scientist draws blood from a baby alligator using a syringe.

Most people wouldn't think of turning to an alligator for help when they are sick. They may not be doctors, but they can still help! Alligators have a liquid in their blood called **serum**. Scientists can remove this serum from their blood. This serum contains **antibodies** that help fight infections, germs, and diseases in humans.

Scientists hope that one day they can turn the serum into pills or creams. They think that these pills and creams will help many people. They have tested the serum with some great results. Scientists think they can help heal burn victims, prevent diabetes, and even cure AIDS. But finding the right amount can be tricky. So far, they have found that too much of the serum can kill humans. So, they need to find the right mixture before it can be sold. But one day, alligator serum just might save human lives.

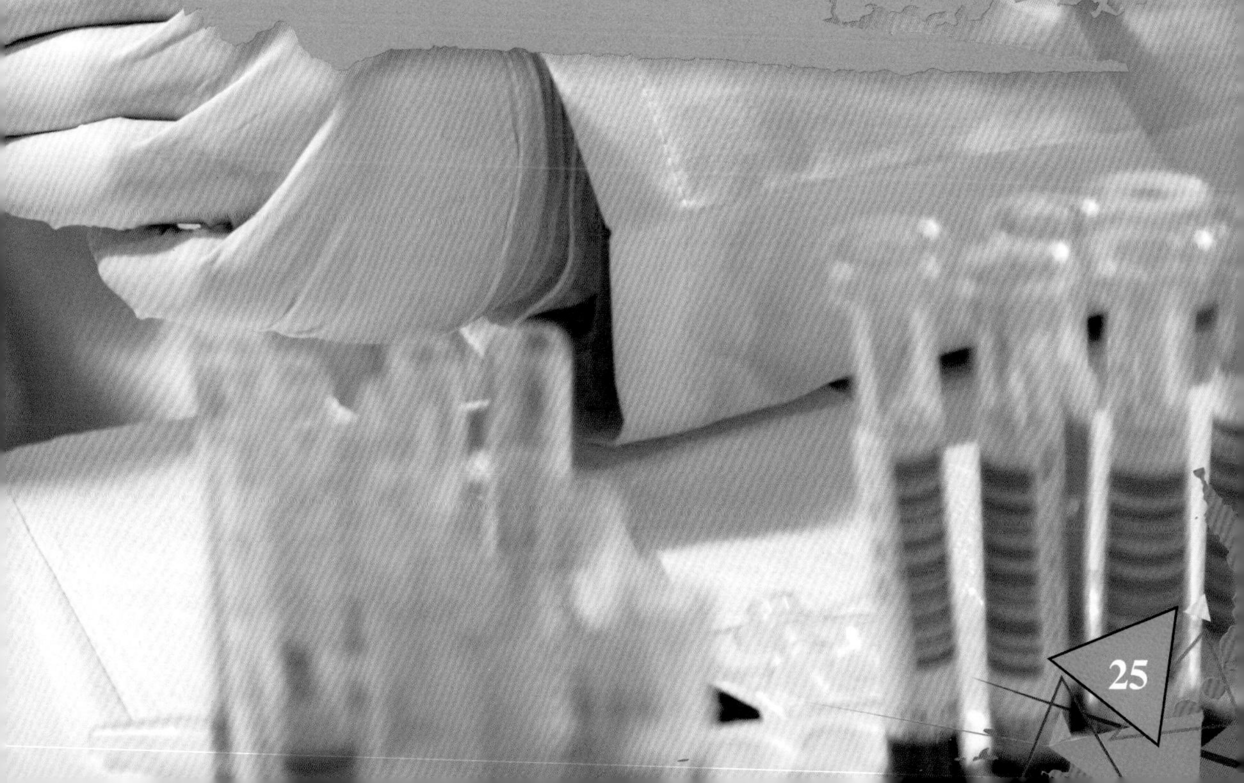

A mother alligator guards her young.

Doing Our Part

Alligators are amazing animals. But, they can be dangerous. After all, they are predators. It is smart to be careful when near them. Any sudden movements will scare them. They will attack if they feel threatened. And no one wants to get caught in a death roll!

Even though alligators are fierce predators, they still need to be protected. We can all do our part to help. It is best for humans to keep a safe distance from alligators. They need space to live in their habitats. That keeps both humans and alligators safe. This way, alligators can be around for millions of more years and can help humans in return!

Problem Solving

Mrs. Edwards is a zookeeper. It is her job to feed, house, and protect animals under her care. It is also her job to host field trips. She is getting ready to welcome some students to the alligator exhibit. After studying alligators at school, they are claiming to be experts! Mrs. Edwards plans to challenge their knowledge of alligator facts. Answer the questions to find out how you would measure up if you were one of the students.

1. Once alligators are about 48 inches long, they are safe from most predators. Hatchlings are about 6 inches long. How many times longer must hatchlings grow to reach this point?

2. In the wild, female alligators lay about 38 eggs each year. Due to predators and other threats, only about 24 of these eggs will hatch. How many eggs will a female lay in 9 years? How many of these eggs will hatch?

3. Four alligators in the zoo are fed about 6 times each month. They each eat about 6 pounds of food at every feeding. How many pounds of food will they eat in one month?

4. The zoo alligators are fed a steady diet. But in the wild, alligators can last for 2 years between feedings. How many days is this? (**Hint:** 1 year = 365 days)

5. Hatchlings weigh about 2 ounces. Adult alligators weigh about 8,000 ounces. How many times larger is an adult than a hatchling?

6. Alligators can go through about 3,000 teeth in a lifetime. How many teeth are the 4 zoo alligators expected to use in their lifetimes?

Glossary

airboat—a flat-bottomed boat powered by a propeller

antibodies—proteins found in blood that help fight infections and diseases

captivity—the state of being kept in a place and not being able to leave

endangered—describing a plant or animal that has become very rare and could die out altogether

extinct—no longer existing

glottis—an opening between vocal cords in the throat

habitat—the type of place where a plant or animal naturally lives or grows

hatchlings—very young animals that have just come out of eggs

murky—very dark or foggy

pods—groups of animals

predators—animals that kill and eat other animals

prey—animals that are hunted and killed

reptiles—animals that have cold blood, lay eggs, and are usually covered with hard parts or scales

serum—a clear liquid found in blood that contains antibodies

species—groups of animals or plants that are similar and can produce young

ton—a unit of measure that equals 2,000 lbs. (910 kg)

Index

Answer Key

Let's Explore Math

page 6:

476 alligators; $238 \times 2 = 476$

page 9:

1. 240 teeth; $80 \times 3 = 240$
2. 480 teeth; $80 \times 6 = 480$

80

80	80	80

80	80	80	80	80	80

page 12:

48 animals; Examples:
$2 \times (10 + 14) = 2 \times 24 = 48$;
$(2 \times 10) + (2 \times 14) = 20 + 28 = 48$

page 15:

1. $25 \times \square = 75$
2. 3; Strategies will vary, but may include using a bar model to show that 3 groups of 25 is 75.

page 21:

Area model shows product of 2,100 lbs.;
$525 \times 4 = 2{,}000 + 80 + 20 = 2{,}100$

page 23:

1. $100 \times 3 = 300$ sq. km;
   $105 \times 3 = 315$ sq. km
2. 735 sq. km; Strategies will vary, but may include using place value, area models, bar models, or equations.

Problem Solving

1. 8 times
2. 342 eggs; 216 eggs will hatch
3. 144 lbs.
4. 730 days
5. 4,000 times
6. 12,000 teeth